D1298959

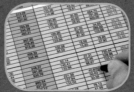

DATABASES: ORGANIZING INFORMATION

GREG ROZA

rosen publishing's
rosen central®

New York

Published in 2011 by The Rosen Publishing Group, Inc.
29 East 21st Street, New York, NY 10010

Copyright © 2011 by The Rosen Publishing Group, Inc.

First Edition

Library of Congress Cataloging-in-Publication Data

Roza, Greg.
Databases: organizing information / Greg Roza. — 1st ed.
    p. cm. — (Digital and information literacy)
Includes bibliographical references and index.
ISBN 978-1-4358-9426-6 (library binding)
ISBN 978-1-4488-0592-1 (pbk)
ISBN 978-1-4488-0605-8 (6-pack)
1. Databases. 2. Relational databases. I. Title.
QA76.9.D32R693 2011
005.75'6–dc22

                                                    2010003046

Manufactured in the United States of America

CPSIA Compliance Information: Batch #S10YA: For further information, contact Rosen Publishing, New York, New York, at 1-800-237-9932.

CONTENTS

INTRODUCTION

Today's computers can efficiently process a great deal of data very quickly, revolutionizing the way that information is both stored and organized. Take libraries, for example. Not that long ago, people used a card catalog to find the books, periodicals, recordings, and other media that they needed at the library. A card catalog is a file cabinet filled with an index card for every resource in the library. The cards are organized alphabetically by author, title, and subject to allow people to easily find the sources that they require. Libraries were organized this way for hundreds of years.

Although some libraries still have a card catalog, it is now much more common for libraries to keep track of their holdings with a computer database called an online public access catalog (OPAC). This is essentially an electronic card catalog that is stored and managed on computers. There are several benefits of using OPAC over a traditional card catalog. As you can probably imagine, a card catalog usually takes up a lot of room, especially in larger libraries. Modern libraries have replaced the card catalog cabinets with smaller computer stations where library patrons can search for books and other resources. OPAC systems can be searched online from anywhere in the world. Furthermore, OPAC systems usually make the search process quicker and more streamlined. They also make it easier to request and reserve materials, pay fines, and even check library events and hours.

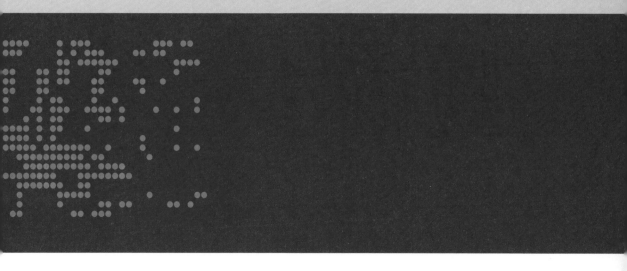

OPAC is just one example of how computer databases have changed our world in recent years. Imagine how difficult it once was for law enforcement officials, doctors, and lawyers to keep records. In these industries, creating, maintaining, and recalling information no longer depends on countless reams of paper and rooms full of file cabinets. All of this has been replaced by digital databases, which can efficiently manage a large amount of interrelated data and organize it as a single unit. Databases allow multiple users throughout an office or company to access important records on their computers.

Nearly every company, organization, and governmental department uses databases to conduct business. It is hard to imagine what our world would be like without them. Today's online retailers, for example, would not be able to function without databases. Simply stated, databases are convenient and powerful tools for organizing information. To really understand how databases work, it is necessary to understand what they are, what they consist of, and how they work to organize information.

Chapter 1

What Is a Database?

atabases are capable of storing vast amounts of data. A
database "processes" the data stored in its files and transforms
it into usable information when the need arises. When something
such as data is processed, it goes through a series of steps (known as a
process) in order to produce, manufacture, or compile a finished product.
For instance, take processed food. Food processing is a series of steps used
to transform edible raw materials into a marketable food product. In many
ways, data processing is similar.

Data and Information

You can think of data as the "raw materials" that a database processes.
Data might include names, addresses, phone numbers, dates, products,
book titles, or Web links. In short, data can include any fact or figure that
an individual, group, or company needs to store and recall.

Taken by itself, a piece of data can have very little meaning. For
example, out of context, the number "14092" has no meaning. Is this

This woman is using a database to search a library catalog. Computer databases have revolutionized the way that data is stored and accessed.

the serial number of an automobile? Is it the population of a city? Does it represent some kind of monetary value? There is no way to know for sure until the data is processed. At that point, the data becomes tangible information.

We use computer programs called database management systems (DBMS) to create and use databases. A DBMS retrieves data from database files and displays it in a useful, meaningful format. Once the number "14092" is processed, it becomes meaningful information: It is the ZIP code

○○○   Online MARC Catalog
◀ ▶ + ⊕ http://www.nara.gov/cgi-bin/starfinder/0?path=marcat.txt&id=demo&pass=&OK=OK   ↻   Q▾ Google
▢ ⊞ Google

Search the NARA Library Online Public Access Catalog

(Submit Search) (Display Search Results) (Clear) (Exit Catalog) (Help)

Records Retrieved: 0   **Max Records to Display** [50 ▴▾]

                    Key Words [   ]
                              ☐ *Use my search operators*

                    Title [   ] (Titles)
                          ☐ *Match exactly as pasted/entered*

        Personal or [   ] (Names)
    Corporate Author
                          ☐ *Match exactly as pasted/entered*

                Subjects [   ] (Subjects)
                          ☐ *Match exactly as pasted/entered*

        Call Number(s) [   ] (Call Nos.)
                          ☐ *Match exactly as pasted/entered*

                Format [   ] (Formats)

    Publication Year from [   ] through [   ]

                          ☐ **Exclude titles on order**

(Submit Search) (Display Search Results) (Clear) (EXIT Catalog)

The National Archives and Records Administration (http://www.nara.gov) stores important U.S. documents, from the Declaration of Independence to census records. Users can search the NARA database for historic documents.

for Lewiston, New York. Although the terms "data" and "information" are very similar, they are often confused in the world of database design. It is important to remember that data are the "raw materials" upon which a database is founded; after data has been processed it becomes information.

Database Management Systems

We would not be able to create and use databases if it weren't for database management systems. There are many different brands of DBMS software. Some of the most common include Microsoft Access, Microsoft SQL, Oracle, and FileMaker Pro. These DBMS use different methods, and they require users to follow different directions. Users often prefer one kind of DBMS over the others. But despite their differences, all DBMS function the same way. They process data into information.

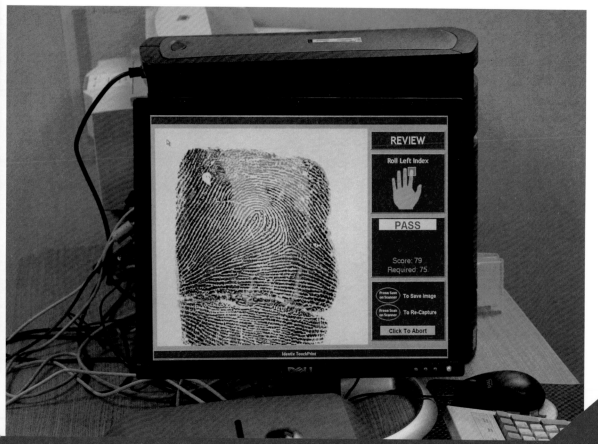

This FBI database stores information on criminals, including their fingerprints. Databases have proven to be invaluable crime-fighting tools in the world of law enforcement.

In order to do this, they use three distinct levels, or layers, of data processing. These layers are known as the physical layer, the logical layer, and the external layer. Collectively, they are called the layers of abstraction.

The Physical Layer

Raw database files are stored in the physical layer of a database. This is the layer that designers create and modify. The physical layer is known as a concrete layer, as it contains actual files that a user can manipulate on a computer. However, in most cases, the typical database user won't ever need to look at these files or understand how they were made. This layer is strictly the domain of the database designer.

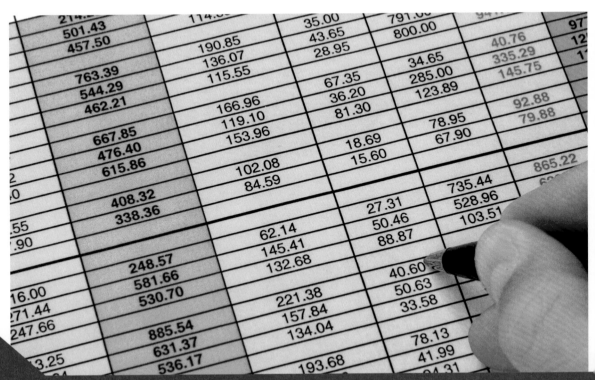

Spreadsheets, such as the one shown here, can be useful when keeping track of money in a checking account or when planning a budget. Spreadsheets consist of a single table.

The Logical Layer

The next layer is the logical layer, which is an abstract layer. This means that it doesn't really exist like the physical files do. The logical layer is a representation of all the information that is included in a database. Part (or all) of the logical layer can be represented using a tree diagram. The logical layer of a database is sometimes known as a schema.

File   Edit   View   Favorites   Tools   Help

DATABASES AND SPREADSHEETS

Databases and Spreadsheets

A spreadsheet is a tool for tracking financial data and solving numerical problems. Spreadsheets are similar to databases, particularly in the way they look: Both databases and spreadsheets are generally presented in table form. However, there are fundamental differences between them.

A spreadsheet is a single, static table that organizes information into columns and rows. It presents the same kind of information to everyone who looks at it. Users can change the information in a spreadsheet, and all users will see these changes when the file is opened.

Most databases are made up of many files of data, rather than a single file. They offer users the ability to ask questions, or queries, in order to find specific information. For example, a bookseller might not only need to know how many books it has in stock from a particular publisher, but also how many of these books were published in the past five years. Or a music collector might want to know how many albums in his or her collection contain a version of the song titled "America the Beautiful"—but only those that were released before 1986. These are functions that a database can accomplish, but which a spreadsheet cannot.

The External Layer

The third layer of a database is called the external layer. This is the layer that the typical user sees after doing a search for information. The information in the external layer is usually displayed as a table. Information in the external layer is constructed from data that exists in the logical layer. The external layer represents a fraction of the total data stored in a database.

Most people who use a database only interact with the external layer. User input at the external layer does not affect the actual structure of the database. For instance, a single database user can save his or her preferred settings in this layer. When a user's copy of the DBMS opens a database, the data is displayed the way the user likes it. This is called a view. Creating a view doesn't change the data on the physical and logical layers. It also doesn't change the views that other users prefer to see when they search a database.

Chapter 2

Tables

Database files store data in tables. In fact, a database is essentially a collection of tables that display the information recalled by a DBMS. A table is a unified collection of data or information that is organized in fields (columns) and records (rows). The objects that are displayed in a table are called entities.

The most commonly used database is the relational database. Relational databases have several distinct benefits over the other kinds of databases. When we talk about database tables, we are mainly referring to relational databases.

Fields and Records

The columns of a database table are called fields. Sometimes they are also known as attributes. Fields are the parts of a database that actually store data. A field represents a single characteristic, or value, of a table. A value is a piece of data, such as a name, price, or serial number, which a user

Many Web sites use databases to enable users to find the information they need. This is the search page for Thomas (http://thomas.loc.gov), a database of federal legislative information administered by the Library of Congress.

needs to keep track of. The data stored as fields in a database can be retrieved and presented as information by a user.

The rows of a database are called records. They also may be called occurrences or tuples. A record is a collection of data related to a specific entity, such as a customer. Each record in a database table displays a single value for each field. For instance, a table that lists fifty customers has fifty records. Each record is made up of the entire set of fields in a table. Each field describes a single aspect of the record.

The simple database example below has three fields: Client ID, First Name, and Last Name. It also has three records, each of which has information related to three unique clients.

CLIENT TABLE

	FIELD 1	FIELD 2	FIELD 3
	Client ID	First Name	Last Name
RECORD 1	443	Jennifer	Roberts
RECORD 2	444	Dan	Smith
RECORD 3	445	Dan	Smith

Database designers often give each person in a database a unique ID number to help avoid identical records. For example, there are two clients named Dan Smith in this table of clients. Having two identical records could cause confusion. To prevent this, each client listed in the database is given a unique ID number. This way, even if two clients have the same name, they can be distinguished by their ID numbers. This ID field is an example of a primary key.

Keys

Keys are one or more fields that help keep information organized. They place certain rules on a field to restrict the types of data that it can contain

Steven Hinrichs, director of the Nebraska Public Health Laboratory, demonstrates a doctor database in his Omaha, Nebraska, laboratory. The database can be used to quickly alert health care workers in the event of a health crisis.

and display. There are several different kinds of keys, but the most important is the primary key.

A primary key is a field or set of fields that uniquely identifies each record in a table. In other words, each record in a primary key is different from all the other records in the database. Most tables use a primary key to help avoid confusion. For example, let's say that the client table example only had two fields: first name and last name. Since there are two Dan Smiths in the table, users would not be able to tell the two records apart. By giving each client a unique ID number, however, users can easily tell the two Dan Smiths apart. The ID field is an example of a primary key. A table may not have more than one primary key.

Another common type of key is the foreign key. A table can have multiple foreign keys. A foreign key is a field or group of fields that corresponds to a primary key in another table of the database.

File   Edit   View   Favorites   Tools   Help

NULL VALUES

Null Values

Database designers use the term "null" or "null value" to represent a missing or unknown value in a field. Null does not mean zero—a zero in a field could represent anything. For instance, it could indicate that there is no money in an account, or that a store is out of a particular product. In other words, a zero in a field still represents a value. A null value, on the other hand, means that information is missing or unavailable. Null values may be included in a table for various reasons. Sometimes the data simply is not available yet. At other times, human error could have led to no values being entered into a particular field.

Null values can cause problems in databases. This is especially true when they are part of a field that includes mathematical operations. For example, let's say that a table includes fields for amount paid, amount owed, and total amount. If there is a null value in one of the first two fields, the values in the last column won't be accurate.

To better understand this, let's once again use the example of the Client Database table. Let's say that the database that contains the client table also has an address table, which would look like this:

ADDRESS TABLE

First Name	Last Name	Address
Jennifer	Roberts	834 Sunset Avenue
Dan	Smith	213 Main Street
Dan	Smith	53 Elm Street

The primary key for the address table is the address field because each address uniquely identifies each record.

However, we still can't be sure which Dan Smith lives at which address. To overcome this confusion, we can use a foreign key. For example, the primary key from the client table (the client ID number) can replace the first and last name fields of the address table. This way, the table lists a unique number instead of listing each client's name.

CLIENT TABLE

Client ID	First Name	Last Name
443	Jennifer	Roberts
444	Dan	Smith
445	Dan	Smith

ADDRESS TABLE

Client ID	Address
443	834 Sunset Avenue
444	213 Main Street
445	53 Elm Street

The client ID column is common to both the client table and the address table. For the address table, the client ID field is called a foreign key because it comes from an outside source. The client ID field creates a "relation" between the two tables (noted by the arrow). A table can have multiple relations simply by adding more foreign key fields to it. This is where the term "relational database" comes from.

Domain

A column's domain is the set of values that are allowed for that particular field. For instance, a field labeled "Cost" would be limited to monetary values. Furthermore, it might be specifically limited to dollar amounts no larger than three digits, or nothing higher than $999. It may also include two decimals to allow for cents. Other examples of domain may include fields that are limited to last names, phone numbers, shirt sizes, and any other specific data necessary for keeping complete records. Applying domain values to a field makes it easier to make changes. It also ensures that all data is treated the same throughout the field.

TEN GREAT QUESTIONS

TO ASK A MULTIMEDIA LIBRARIAN

1. What kind of school projects could I use a database for?

2. Can I access LexisNexis from the school library?

3. What is the best way to learn how to use a particular DBMS?

4. What are the best books on database design?

5. What kind of classes can I take in high school that will be useful for learning how to build databases?

6. Can I go to college for database design?

7. How do I design a database that meets the needs of its user?

8. What are the benefits of using relational databases over other types of databases?

9. How important is it to learn database structures other than relational databases?

10. What kinds of jobs can I get if I know how to design databases?

Chapter 3

Breaking Down Databases

Learning to use or create databases can seem very daunting at first. As with any new subject, it helps to learn about basic database terminology before proceeding. Familiarizing oneself with the important parts of a database, and the functions of a database, can make understanding the process by which databases organize information much easier.

Database Files

Databases store their data in files. Depending on the DBMS, a file may contain a table, or it may contain an entire database. When a user first begins to create a database, he or she must create a new database file. This provides a blank slate to begin designing. Once data has been added to a file, the user can save and close it; the data will still be there when the file is opened again. A database may contain dozens or even hundreds of files.

Identity		Primary Key
		PSC002935443

Title

Subtitle

	ISBN		

Product Type

Status

Season

Schedule

Revisions

A book publisher might use a database like the one shown here to organize information regarding its products. This database was made using the FileMaker Pro DBMS.

You might think of database files as physical pieces of paper stored neatly in a file cabinet. If you need to read a file, you open the right file drawer, find the right file folder, and select the file you are looking for. Database management systems work in a similar way. When a user needs information, the DBMS opens the correct files and uses the data to compile the exact information that the user requested.

Asking Questions

Database users find the information they need by asking specific questions. The questions a database user asks are called queries. The answers a user receives come in the form of tables filled with information.

For example, someone who owns a DVD collection might ask his or her database, "How many movies do I own starring the actor John Smith?" The database would respond to this question by displaying a table with information that will answer the user's question. The user could limit the results even further by making the question more specific, such as, "How many movies do

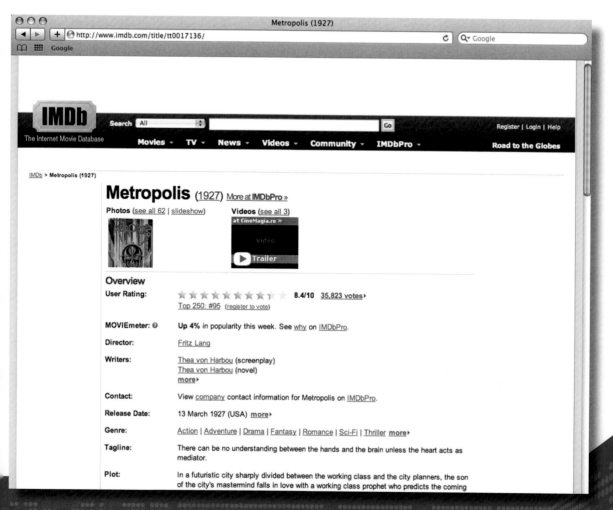

The Internet Movie Database (http://www.imdb.com) is a popular database containing abundant information on nearly every film and television show ever made. Anyone can search the database by entering a title, actor, director, or other criteria.

I own starring the actor John Smith, made between 2004 and 2008?" The results would be a smaller table showing even more specific information.

Queries can be as specific or as general as a user needs them to be. For example, perhaps the DVD collector wants the list in alphabetical order. Or perhaps he or she wants it in chronological order, or limited to movies made by a specific production company. Queries allow users to get the exact information that they are looking for.

Structured Query Language

When using a relational DBMS, a user can't just ask a query in plain, everyday language. It must be entered using Structured Query Language, or SQL. SQL is a computer language designed to create, change, and recall data. Making queries is the most common use for SQL. While SQL language may seem complicated at first, users often pick it up quickly.

To use SQL, users must know several search terms called select statements, or commands. Select statements determine how the information will be processed and displayed. Specific select statements include "where," "group by," and "order by." Knowing SQL and understanding how to use it allows database users to find the exact information they need at a moment's notice. SQL is also used to design databases. SQL commands are sorted into two categories: Data Definition Language (DDL) commands and Data Manipulation Language (DML) commands.

DDL Commands

Commands that are used to create and destroy databases and database elements are called DDL commands. One of the most important DDL commands is CREATE. For example, if a user was starting a study group, he or she might want to create a database to keep track of members. To create a new database, the user would input a create command into the DBMS:

CREATE DATABASE group members

This command creates a blank database named "group members." Next, the user will need to create tables within the database. To create a new table, a user might input a command such as:

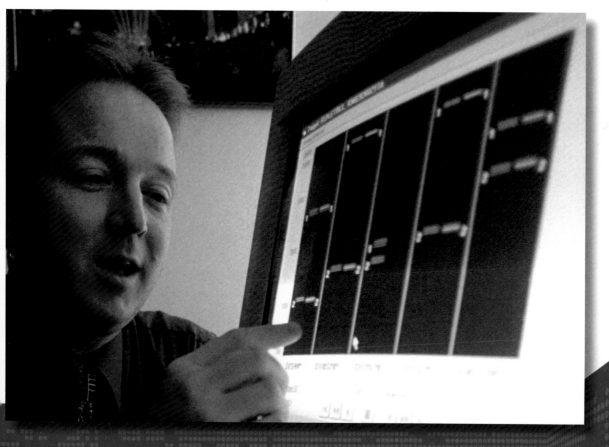

David Coffman of the Florida Department of Law Enforcement uses a DNA database to match identical DNA samples. This would be nearly impossible without database technology.

CREATE TABLE contact information (first name, last name, address, phone number).

This command would create a blank table with four fields. Other important DDL commands include USE, which allows a user to select a specific table to work with; and DROP, which allows a user to completely delete an entire table.

File   Edit   View   Favorites   Tools   Help

DOING RESEARCH

Doing Research

Databases give students access to a great deal of useful information. For instance, the LexisNexis database archives magazines, newspapers, periodicals, and other content that is extremely useful for students and researchers. Many academic and municipal libraries are connected to LexisNexis, allowing students to access a massive amount of data free of charge. Rather than SQL, LexisNexis utilizes a query language called Enterprise Control Language (ECL). Databases like Academic Onefile and JSTOR archive a massive collection of academic journals and are generally used by college students and professional researchers who need specialized information. People doing research anywhere in the world can search these databases for the information that they need.

DML Commands

Commands that are used to add, modify, and retrieve data are called DML commands. The most common DML command is SELECT. This command allows users to find the exact information they need. For example, if a user input the command "SELECT group members," the results would be a table containing all group members and the relevant information about each member. Some DML commands help narrow query results. If a user just wants a list of members' phone numbers, he or she would input:

        SELECT phone number
        FROM group members

If the user needs a record of the group members over a certain age, he or she would input:

```
SELECT *
FROM group members
WHERE age > 15
```

This literally says: "Select only the people from the group member table who are older than fifteen." Another important DML command is INSERT, which allows users to add new data, such as a new group member, to the database.

Views

When a user makes a query, the DBMS processes data, converting it into useable information. That information is presented to the user as a table called a view. Views are different from the tables that are used to store data in a database. This is because the information exists only as the answer to a query. The information cannot be altered in view form.

Views are sometimes called virtual tables. The word "virtual" refers to something created by a computer that is not real. A virtual table is one that has no existence beyond its use as an answer to a query. It doesn't really exist as part of the database in the same way that a table containing data exists in a database file.

MYTHS & FACTS

MYTH SQL is too difficult to learn.

FACT Although SQL can look complex to people who have never used it, many people find that it doesn't take too long to get the hang of it. It is important to learn the SQL commands and the way that queries and directions are formatted.

MYTH All databases are essentially the same.

FACT There are many different kinds of databases. Relational databases are the most common, but other types of databases, such as network databases, can also be very useful for specific functions. Depending on the kind and amount of data that they need to process, databases can be of varying complexity. A simple relational database might be adequate for the needs of individuals or small businesses. A large multinational corporation might require several different types of extremely complex databases.

MYTH

FACT A person needs to go to school to learn how to design databases.
Many universities that offer computer degrees have database courses. However, college isn't a person's only option when it comes to learning how to design databases. Many people are able to teach themselves simply by using the software. Others thrive with more structured guidance. There are many reputable online database courses, and many of them are free. Likewise, there are dozens of books on the topic.

Chapter 4

Relational Databases

There are many kinds of databases in the world. Not all database systems use the table format described in this book. In fact, a database can be loosely defined as being any collection of interrelated data. At one time, all databases were "flat." Information about a topic was stored as a single file. The information was presented as a long list, perhaps separated by special characters. With so many items listed in a single text file, individual pieces of data could be difficult to find.

When we talk about databases in the modern world, we are almost always talking about computer databases. Although this book primarily discusses relational databases and their structure, there are many other types of databases. These database structures all have their uses. However, no database is as versatile, or as popular, as the relational database.

The Database Revolution

In 1970, IBM researcher E. F. Codd revolutionized the world of digital databases by inventing the relational database. Instead of simple, inflexible flat

This 1973 photograph shows an IBM computer center in Milwaukee, Wisconsin. Today, much of the data stored in this room full of computers could fit on a single computer.

files, Codd suggested storing data in tables that could be linked to each other. Tables made it much easier for users to find and read data, and this system gave users more options when searching for information. For the first time, database users could sort information based on a specific field, and they could reorganize data in any way that they wanted.

The tables in relational databases can share associations, or relations, with each other. The objects or entities that are stored as data in a

database often interact with each other. For example, when a customer buys a product, he or she establishes a relationship with that product. The customer is one entity, and the product is the other. In the world of data-bases, these associations are known as one-to-one relationships. Of course, one entity can have associations with many other entities. A customer can buy several products, for example. When tracked in a database, these associations are called one-to-many relationships. Besides one-to-one and

The formerly communist East German secret police kept extensive records on East German citizens on data cards, shown here. Prior to the existence of digital databases, data had to be stored in bulky physical files.

one-to-many relationships, a database can also track many-to-one and many-to-many relationships.

Designing a Relational Database

Here is a simple example of database design. Let's say that Samantha was just hired by a music school to create and maintain a database. Samantha asks her new boss what he would like to keep track of, and he gives her the following criteria: member names, the types of lessons available, and the cost of each lesson. He also gives her personal data regarding the school's current members, some of whom take more than one class.

Samantha starts by opening her DBMS. She inputs the following DDL command: "CREATE DATABASE Member Lessons." This creates a new database file.

Next, she begins to create a new table with the following DDL command: "CREATE TABLE member lessons (Member, Lesson 1, Cost 1, Lesson 2, Cost 2)." This command creates a table with five fields. (It is important to note that the command would probably contain other criteria, such as the domain values for the cost columns. But for our purposes, we will leave those criteria out.) This is what Samantha's initial table looks like:

MEMBER LESSONS

Member	Lesson 1	Cost 1	Lesson 2	Cost 2
Kelly O'Hare	Tuba	$30		
Brian Smith	Oboe	$25	Music Theory	$15
Carol Barker	Piano	$20		
Brian Smith	Piano	$20	Voice	$20

Samantha's database is off to a good start, but she sees a problem. There are two members named Brian Smith. How will her boss be able to tell which Brian Smith owes dues for oboe and music theory lessons, and which Brian Smith owes dues for piano and voice lessons?

To correct this problem, Samantha gives each member his own special code. Then she replaces the member field with one labeled ID#.

MEMBER LESSONS

ID#	Lesson 1	Cost 1	Lesson 2	Cost 2
1	Tuba	$30		
2	Oboe	$25	Music Theory	$15
3	Piano	$20		
4	Piano	$20	Voice	$20

Now each record (or row) on the table is unique because each has its own ID number. The ID# field is the primary key. As we have already learned, a primary key is a field that uniquely identifies each record in a table.

However, Samantha notices that there is another problem. While a computer may have no problem organizing the ID numbers, it is not likely that a user reading this table will be able to identify a member by his or her ID number. So Samantha creates a member information table using the DDL command: "CREATE TABLE Member Information (Member, ID#, Address, Phone Number, Amount Due)." The result is the following table:

MEMBER INFORMATION

ID#	Member	Address	Phone Number	Amount Due
1	Kelly O'Hare	431 Elm	555-4915	$0.00
2	Brian Smith	9984 Parkhurst	555-2208	$0.00
3	Carol Barker	12B Glenwood	555-3945	$0.00
4	Brian Smith	774 Main	555-8388	$20.00

Once she has created both tables, Samantha links them together based on their common field: ID#. The ID number field is the primary key for both tables. At this point, Samantha's database has become a relational database.

OTHER TYPES OF DATABASES

Other Types of Databases

There are many kinds of databases besides relational databases. Other database types include hierarchical databases and network databases.

As their name suggests, hierarchical databases are arranged in a hierarchy. A hierarchy is a system of grouping things where one object is on the top, and there are others branching out below it. For instance, a family tree denotes a hierarchy. At the top of the family tree are two people, and moving downward, the rest of the family spreads out from them. A piece of data higher in the hierarchy is known as a "parent," and a piece of data branching off of the parent is known as a "child." In the hierarchical model, a "parent" can have multiple "children." However, each "child" is specific to the "parent" it branches off from; it cannot branch off from more than one "parent."

Network databases are arranged somewhat similarly to hierarchical databases. However, the way that they organize information is more flexible. Like hierarchical databases, network databases organize data in the form of "parent" and "child" relationships. However, unlike hierarchical databases, network databases allow each piece of "child" data to have multiple "parents." The relationship between different items in a hierarchical database is always organized from the top downward, but it does not have to be in a network database.

Things are going well so far, but Samantha is not done yet. She decides that the lessons table could cause some problems in the future. She notes that some fields are blank, or contain null values. Also, what if a member decides that he or she wants to add a third or fourth lesson?

There is no room for that in the database. Samantha decides to modify the lesson table.

MEMBER LESSONS

ID#	Lesson	Cost
1	Tuba	$30
2	Oboe	$25
2	Music Theory	$15
3	Piano	$20
4	Piano	$20
4	Voice	$20

Samantha has simplified the table. In this case, the ID# field and the Lesson field combine to make the primary key. Each student, represented by an ID#, can only take a lesson once. Together, the two fields uniquely identify each record.

There is one last thing bothering Samantha. What if the lesson costs change? If the cost for piano lessons went up to $25, she would have to go through the table and change every instance where that cost changed. To avoid this problem, Samantha decides to modify the member lesson table once again and create a third table.

MEMBER LESSONS

ID#	Lesson
1	Tuba
2	Oboe
2	Music Theory
3	Piano
4	Piano

COST TABLE

Lesson	Cost
Tuba	$30
Oboe	$25
Music Theory	$15
Piano	$20
Voice	$20

You may have already used several databases without even knowing it. For example, these students are using computer databases to search for books and other resources to use for research projects.

The two tables that Samantha created have a relationship. They share lesson data. This is the field that links the two tables together. Should the price of tuba lessons ever go up to $35, Samantha would only need to change the cost once on the cost table. Since the cost table is linked to the lesson table, all instances of the price change would be automatically updated. This simple example demonstrates the power and versatility of relational databases.

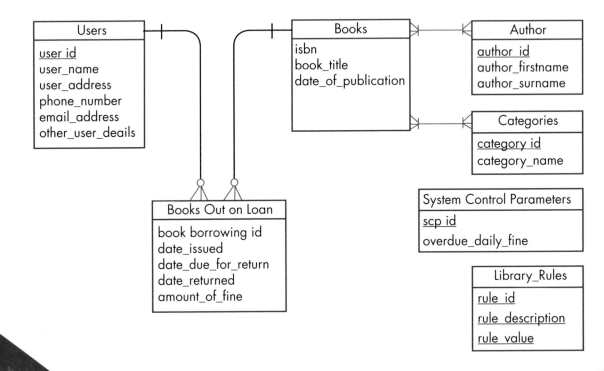

Shown here is a map, or schema, of a library database from DatabaseAnswers.org. Notice that the arrows show which tables share relations.

Schema: Visualizing Databases

By now, it is probably getting easier to picture what a database actually looks like, or how the different parts fit together to form a useful whole. Relational databases are complex webs of tables, fields, and the relationships between them. The entire structure of a database is called its schema.

A database schema can be represented by a physical diagram showing how the tables are connected. A schema for the example in the previous section would look something like this:

MEMBER INFORMATION

ID#	Member	Address	Phone Number	Amount Due

MEMBER LESSONS

ID#	Lesson

COST TABLE

Lesson	Cost

This schema helps us understand the relations in Samantha's database. The arrows in this schema show which fields are related. At this point, the schema shown here represents the logical layer of database design. A person can't physically see a database schema when he or she is working on the database. But schema can help people visualize the structure of a database that they are building. Keep in mind, however, that this is just the start. To finish her database, Samantha will undoubtedly need to consider more criteria, such as the products that are for sale in the music shop, methods of payment, and late fees, to name just a few.

Moving On

Although designing databases can seem complicated, it is certainly not impossible. With a little practice, almost anyone can use databases and learn SQL. In fact, some DBMS allow users to issue commands by clicking buttons or icons, rather than issuing the commands in SQL. Once a user learns the basics of database use and design, he or she can create databases, modify and add to them, and search them for a wide range of facts and figures. Learning about databases can allow a person to take advantage of these undeniably useful and convenient tools.

GLOSSARY

abstract Not relating to concrete objects or actions.

data The "raw materials" that a database processes. Before it is processed, data has no real meaning.

database management system (DBMS) A computer program that allows users to create, modify, and search a database.

domain The values that are allowed for a particular field.

entity An object displayed in a database. An entity can be any real-world person, place, observation, product, or transaction.

external Existing outside of the main body or group.

field A column of a database table. A field represents a single characteristic, or value, of a table.

foreign key One or more fields that are related to values in fields in another table.

hierarchy A group that is organized in ranks.

information Processed data that is displayed in a table, called a view, for database users to see.

input To insert data or commands into a computer program.

interrelated Describing a relationship in which each object depends on, or is affected by, the other objects.

layer of abstraction One of three layers of data processing used by a DBMS.

logical Based on clear, rational thought.

network An interrelated system of people, things, or ideas.

null Missing or unknown data in a database field.

primary key The field of a database table that uniquely identifies all the records.

query An SQL statement that extracts data from a database.

record A row of a database table; a collection of data related to a specific entity, such as a customer.

relation A connection shared between two entities or tables in a database.

schema A physical representation of the abstract data stored in a database.

spreadsheet A computer program that displays numerical data in tables. These tables are made up of small boxes called cells, which contain data. Changing the data in one cell can cause the recalculation of data in other cells.

static Not moving or changing.

unique Being the only one of a kind.

view A table shown after a database user makes a query. A view is also called a virtual table.

FOR MORE INFORMATION

Association for Computing Machinery (ACM)
2 Penn Plaza
New York, NY 10121
Web site: http://www.acm.org
(800) 342-6626
The largest international educational and scientific computing society, the
    ACM has more than 170 chapters worldwide.

Computer History Museum
1401 N. Shoreline Boulevard
Mountain View, CA 94043
(650) 810-1010
Web site: http://www.computerhistory.org
This museum is dedicated to preserving the history of computing.

Just Think
39 Mesa Street
Suite 106
San Francisco, CA 94129
(415) 561-2900
Web site: http://justthink.org
This organization is dedicated to providing young people with media
    literacy skills.

Media Awareness Network
1500 Merivale Road, 3rd Floor
Ottawa, ON K2E 6Z5
Canada
(613) 224-7721

Web site: http://www.media-awareness.ca
The Media Awareness Network is devoted to promoting media and
    digital literacy.

National Archives and Records Administration (NARA)
8601 Adelphi Road
College Park, MD 20740-6001
(866) 272-6272
Web site: http://www.archives.gov
The NARA is a federal database that stores important and historic
    U.S. documents.

Web Sites

Due to the changing nature of Internet links, Rosen Publishing has developed
an online list of Web sites related to the subject of this book. This site is
updated regularly. Please use this link to access the list:

http://www.rosenlinks.com/dil/data

FOR FURTHER READING

Beaulieu, Alan. *Learning SQL*. Sebastopol, CA: O'Reilly Media, 2009.

Beighley, Lynn. *Head First SQL*. Sebastopol, CA: O'Reilly Media, 2007.

Churcher, Clare. *Beginning Database Design: From Novice to Professional*. Berkeley, CA: Apress, 2007.

Faroult, Stephane. *The Art of SQL*. Sebastopol, CA: O'Reilly Media, 2006.

Forda, Ben. *Teach Yourself SQL in 10 Minutes*. Don Mills, ON, Canada: Pearson Canada, 2004.

Oppel, Andrew. *Databases Demystified*. Emeryville, CA: McGraw-Hill/Osborne Media, 2004.

Oppel, Andrew. *SQL Demystified*. Emeryville, CA: McGraw-Hill/Osborne Media, 2005.

Petersen, John V. *Absolute Beginner's Guide to Databases*. Don Mills, ON, Canada: Pearson Canada, 2002.

Pratt, Phillip J. *A Guide to SQL*. Boston, MA: Course Technology, 2008.

Rob, Peter, and Carlos Coronel. *Database Systems: Design, Implementation, and Management*. Boston, MA: Course Technology, 2007.

Takahashi, Mana. *The Manga Guide to Databases*. Tokyo, Japan: Ohmsha, Ltd., and No Starch Press, 2009.

Taylor, Allen G. *Database Development for Dummies*. Foster City, CA: IDG Books Worldwide, Inc., 2001.

Taylor, Allen G. *SQL for Dummies*. Hoboken, NJ: Wiley Publishing, Inc., 2006.

Viescas, John L. *SQL Queries for Mere Mortals*. Upper Saddle River, NJ: Pearson Education, 2008.

Ward, Patricia, and George Dafoulas. *Database Management Systems*. Florence, KY: Cengage Learning, 2008.

Whitehorn, Mark, and Bill Marklyn. *Inside Relational Databases with Examples in Access*. New York, NY: Springer, 2006.

BIBLIOGRAPHY

Chappel, Mike. "SQL Fundamentals." About.com. Retrieved December 4, 2009 (http://databases.about.com/od/sql/a/sqlfundamentals.htm).

Connolly, Thomas M., and Carolyn E. Begg. *Database Systems: A Practical Approach to Design, Implementation, and Management*. Reading, MA: Addison-Wesley, 2002.

Forda, Ben. *Teach Yourself SQL in 10 Minutes*. Don Mills, ON, Canada: Pearson Canada, 2004.

Gilfillan, Ian. "Introduction to Relational Databases." *Database Journal*, June 24, 2004. Retrieved November 30, 2009 (http://www.databasejournal.com/sqletc/article.php/26861_1469521_1/Introduction-to-Relational-Databases.htm).

Hernandez, Michael J. *Database Design for Mere Mortals*. Reading, MA: Addison-Wesley, 2003.

Oppel, Andrew. *Databases: A Beginner's Guide*. New York, NY: McGraw-Hill, 2009.

SQLCourse.com. "SQL Courses." Retrieved December 6, 2009 (http://sqlcourse.com/intro.html).

Stephens, Rod. *Beginning Database Design Solutions*. Hoboken, NJ: Wiley Publishing, Inc., 2009.

Tahaghoghi, Seyed M. M., and Hugh Williams. *Learning MySQL*. Sebastopol, CA: O'Reilly Media, 2006.

Vines, Rose. "Databases: Step-by-step Guides to Using Databases." GeekGirls.com. Retrieved December 2, 2009 (http://www.geekgirls.com/menu_databases.htm).

INDEX

About the Author

Greg Roza has been creating educational materials for schools and libraries for ten years. He has a master's degree from SUNY Fredonia. Roza lives in Hamburg, New York, with his wife, Abigail, and their children, Autumn, Lincoln, and Daisy.

Photo Credits

Designer: Nicole Russo; Photo Researcher: Cindy Reiman